# FIELD MANUAL FOR THE BROKEN

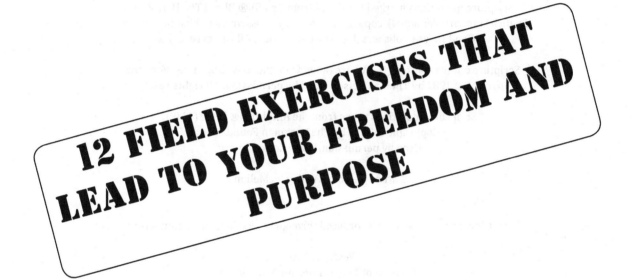

**12 FIELD EXERCISES THAT LEAD TO YOUR FREEDOM AND PURPOSE**

MARYANN TRAINER

AUTHOR OF *BROKEN NO MORE: I AM BECAUSE HE IS*

WESTBOW
PRESS®
A DIVISION OF THOMAS NELSON
& ZONDERVAN

Scripture quotations are taken from the Holy Bible, New Living Translation, copyright
©1996, 2004, 2007, 2013, 2015 by Tyndale House Foundation. Used by permission of
Tyndale House Publishers, Inc., Carol Stream, Illinois 60188. All rights reserved.

Scripture quotations taken from the New American Standard Bible® (NASB), Copyright © 1960, 1962, 1963,
1968, 1971, 1972, 1973, 1975, 1977, 1995 by The Lockman Foundation.Used by permission. www.Lockman.org

Scripture quotations marked (NIV) are taken from the Holy Bible, New International Version®, NIV®. Copyright
© 1973, 1978, 1984, 2011 by Biblica, Inc.™ Used by permission of Zondervan. All rights reserved worldwide.

Scripture quotations marked (ESV) are fromthe ESV® Bible (The Holy Bible,
English Standard Version®), copyright © 2001 by Crossway, a publishing ministry
of Good News Publishers. Used by permission. All rights reserved.

Scripture quotes marked (NKJV) are taken from the New King James Version®.
Copyright © 1982 by Thomas Nelson. Used by permission. All rights reserved.

Scripture quotations taken from the Amplified® Bible (AMP),
Copyright © 2015 by The Lockman Foundation
Used by permission. www.Lockman.org

Author photo by Ashley McMellon


WestBow Press books may be ordered through booksellers or by contacting:

WestBow Press
A Division of Thomas Nelson & Zondervan
1663 Liberty Drive
Bloomington, IN 47403
www.westbowpress.com
1 (866) 928-1240

ISBN: 978-1-5127-5504-6 (sc)
ISBN: 978-1-5127-5505-3 (e)

Library of Congress Control Number: 2016914317

Print information available on the last page.

WestBow Press rev. date: 12/19/2019

# Note to Reader

This Field Manual has been specifically designed by Maryann Trainer, President of Maryann Trainer Counseling Inc. and Founder of Broken No More Ministries, to accompany each attendee at a Broken No More Boot Camp, Trainer Counseling Inc. sessions and small groups with a trained leader. Portions of this Field Manual may seem incomplete or non-sequential. This is by design, as Boot Camp attendees, counseling clients and trained small group leaders, you will receive additional instructions from Maryann Trainer or a certified leader using Maryann Trainer Counseling Incorporated materials.

If you have questions about becoming a trained group leader or would like Maryann Trainer to speak or provide training for your organization, please email TrainerCounseling@gmail.com .

# Acknowledgments

Thank you to our military men and women who have served and sacrificed their lives for our freedom. Your experiences in battle and testimonies have paved the way for me to write a manual by implementing and integrating military war tactics with a spiritual perspective. The spiritual war is real, and my passion is to share vital tools to win the spiritual war and live in freedom.

Thank you to all those in the Army of God who have sacrificed countless hours on the battlefield to rescue the oppressed. God sees you. Well done, good and faithful soldiers!

Thank you to hundreds I have counseled and led through Boot Camps. Your lives and testimonies inspire me to keep moving forward with a "call to arms" even when the battle is fierce. Your tears, fears, and victories have paved the way for this much-needed Field Manual. I see a hopeful future because of your battlefield specialization.

Thank you to my church family. You inspire me to be better. Your prayers, encouragement, love, and support have been a refuge for me when I find myself wounded in battle. Without stating names, you know who you are.

To my children, Ashley and Jacob, you are the future generation. You have taught me how to war on your behalf. You are worth fighting for. I pray to position you for great victory in Christ. You inspired me to write this in hopes that you never are on the field without His armor. I am proud to be your mom.

*Maryann Trainer*

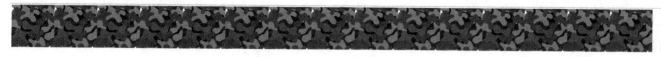

# Dedication

This workbook is dedicated to my mom. God called you home during the editing of this manual, but your story of addiction, mental illness, homelessness, and death stirred a passion in me to help the broken. My pain, alcoholism, captivity, devastation, and great loss have become an inspiration to set captives free in Christ. I promise to use our life story as a platform to the power of Jesus. You are free now.

# Contents

# Introduction

Are you tired? Do you feel defeated in this life? Are you physically exhausted? Is everyday life a struggle? Maybe you cannot get out of bed, or maybe you believe that your life is a mistake. Have you ever asked the questions "How on earth did I get here?" or "Where is God?" Have you ever said, "This was not my plan" or "I had a dream, but somewhere along the path of brokenness, rejection, fear, betrayal, addiction, and abuse, I have lost my way and lost my dream?" Or this thought, "It's too late for me, I have nowhere to go."

If so, you are holding the Field Manual that will empower you to again stand up, to again feel motivated, and to start fighting an enemy—an enemy you may not have known was after you.

You may have never been addressed as a soldier, but from this point forward, that is how I will address you. You have probably been called many things in your life: "worthless, useless, weak, or not good enough." However, I am here to show you the truth, and the truth is that, as a Believer in Christ, you belong to an army of war heroes and you amount to far more than the lies you may have heard prior to opening up this Field Manual.

Maybe this Field Manual is your last resort, your last cry for help and hope. You are desperate and broken and just want to be free from all the pain and the confusion. Is the battle killing you? I have been exactly where you are.

Let me share a scripture that may help awaken you to the battle you are facing. I quote *Ephesians 6:12 (NIV)*, which says, *"For our struggle is not against flesh and blood, but against the rulers, against the authorities, against the powers of this dark world and against the spiritual forces of evil in the heavenly realms."* What if I told you that you were in a spiritual battle? What if Satan is real? What if I told you he is the father of lies and he fills our head daily with negative thoughts? What if I told you he comes to kill, steal, and destroy you? What if he is after you, your family, and your children? What would you do? The Bible says he comes like a lion seeking whom he can devour. *"Be alert and of sober mind. Your enemy the devil prowls around like a roaring lion looking for someone to devour"* (1 Peter 5:8 NIV). If this is true,

it sounds like we are in a war for our lives—family and generations to come. This battle is often termed "spiritual warfare."

You may be asking yourself, "How do I win this battle?" What if I could give you a shield and armor that would guarantee victory over Satan in your life? I hope your combat boots are ready, because this deployment is going to change your life. You are about to wear such armor!

# How to Use this Field Manual

What is a field manual? Militaries often supply their troops with various field manuals that are meant to be read and reviewed on the battlefield. Without the luxury and safety of a classroom back in their home country, soldiers can turn to a field manual when information is needed quickly. Field manuals typically have fewer pages than instructional books, and topics range from how to perform maintenance on a weapon to survival and evasion and operations in certain terrain features. In war zones today, you may still find field manuals in rucksacks, combat vehicles, and any number of other places where soldiers can open the pages quickly, be reminded of the procedures and tactics, and then get back to the fight. Over time and use, worn field manuals would be lovingly repaired with duct tape or wire to ensure the pages continue to be accessible. Interestingly, old US Army Field Manuals once contained Hymns and Prayers for soldiers to reflect on.

This Field Manual is written with much of the same intent. In it, you will find the procedures needed to get your fighting gear back together, focus your scattered and emotional brain, and then stand back up and fight.

The procedures for using this manual are straightforward.

Step #1: Duck! The barrages of life are coming fast and you need to carve out a few hours or days to complete this manual.

Step #2: Follow the steps in order from 1 to 12. Do not skip any, and do not modify the process. The steps are designed to build upon one another.

Step #3: Get up and get back into the fight. Now that you are back in shape, look around for fellow soldiers who need this training. Grab them before it is too late for them.

Now continue reading the next few pages before you begin the first exercise. Don't skip to the first step yet. Read everything!

# What to Expect

Trainer Counseling has performed these exact steps at counseling Boot Camps for countless participants and for individual clients. In nearly every case, people emerge reinvigorated, realigned with God's purposes, and fully equipped for victorious spiritual warfare.

The twelve exercises will open your eyes to see things you may not have seen before, and to shine some light into areas that may be pretty dark. You need to commit to finishing all twelve steps, and do not skip or modify any of the content. Let us say it again: You must **_commit_** to finishing all twelve steps. Otherwise, put this manual down and go watch some mind-numbing crap on TV or the Web that will gain you nothing and ensure that your tomorrow will look just like your yesterday.

Note that some of the exercises require you to handwrite letters, so make sure you have pen and paper ready.

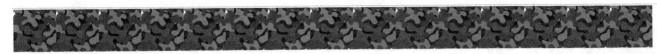

# Legal Stuff

We must state the following, so bear with us here: This Field Manual is designed to assist you in discovering that freedom in Christ is yours. We believe that after completing these intense exercises you will walk in victory, not defeat. However, we want you to understand this Field Manual cannot, and is not designed to, replace professional counseling. This Field Manual provides structure, guidance, and techniques to assist you in spiritual warfare training and freedom in Christ Jesus. Depending on your situation, you may need additional assistance from a church pastor or professional counselor.

## Citizenship Check

Before we move further, I have a very important question.

Are you saved? Saved as in the Christian sense of accepting Jesus Christ as your personal Savior? Some call it "born again." I ask this question with great respect and urgency. This is the first question I ask in session, as your answer is vital for your freedom in Christ. If you are not saved in Christ, you are not His soldier yet and you do not possess His power through the Holy Spirit to fight your battles. If we, in this Field Manual, are declaring war against the enemy, how can you win if you do not have the sword of the Spirit as your sword? The most unethical decision I could make as a counselor is sending you into battle against the enemy while knowing you are without a sword and armor. That would be suicide! If you have not given your life to Jesus Christ, salvation would be the first step in winning this war.

What does salvation mean? The Bible states in **Romans 10:9 (NIV), _"If you declare with your mouth, 'Jesus is Lord,' and believe in your heart that God raised him from the dead, you will be saved."_**

If you are ready to surrender your life to Christ, to be handed a sword that never ends in defeat, to war and win for the generation to come, and to become a war hero, you need to pray the prayer below—preferably out loud. If you have already surrendered your life to Christ, please renew your commitment today with this prayer as well. Remember to read this prayer out loud, as we are to _confess_ with our mouth that Jesus is Lord.

By the way, you cannot claim that someone else has you covered in this area. Salvation is individual and personal between God and you. If your grandmother was a great Christian, you are not automatically covered. If your family had you dedicated as a newborn, sorry, this doesn't work either. You were not even conscious of the fact that you needed a bathroom, much less a Savior. If you were taught anything about Jesus that is contrary to the Bible, then you probably have been introduced to a different personality than the Christ that walked the sandy roads of Israel over 2,000 years ago. Are we being too specific here about Christ? Nope. If you get this part wrong and hang your eternal fate in the wrong hands, then you've stepped out on the wrong foot from day one.

# Soldier Commissioning

Say this prayer out loud:

*Lord Jesus Christ, thank you for dying on the cross. I believe wholeheartedly that you were sent to die on the cross for my sins. I acknowledge that I am a sinner, I have sinned against You, and I need Your forgiveness. Forgive me, Lord, make me new, and make me like You. Please fill me with Your Holy Spirit. Hand me the Sword of the Spirit, Lord, the sword that promises me victory over loss and darkness as well as freedom for my life, my family, and generations to come. Please renew my mind and my heart. Make me a war hero. Help me to war and win and break generational sin. Show me the power of Your Word and how to use it in battle. Thank you, Lord Jesus, for setting me free. In Jesus' Name I pray. Amen.*

Do you believe Jesus is Lord? Do you believe that God raised Christ from the dead? Did you invite the Holy Spirit to come live in you? Did you recommit your life to Christ? If you said yes to all of the above, then you are a child of God and a soldier in the Army of God. You are finally ready to war and win!

Please state now out loud, "I am a child of God and whom the Son sets free is free indeed!"

Congratulations, and welcome to the Kingdom of God! Your name has now been written in the Lamb's Book of Life! The Word of God says in *Malachi 3:16 (NIV),*

*Then those who feared the LORD talked with each other, and the LORD listened and heard. A scroll of remembrance was written in his presence concerning those who feared the LORD and honored his name.*

In *Revelation 3:5 (NIV),* the Word states,

*The one who is victorious will, like them, be dressed in white. I will never blot out the name of that person from the book of life, but will acknowledge that name before my Father and his angels.*

Write it down! On this _____ day of _____, in the year _____, I have been saved, and today is my new spiritual birthday. And all of heaven rejoices!

## Note

Not buying it? Think all of this Jesus stuff isn't for you? Not ready to get all Christian weird? Okay. We understand. We suggest you stop here and think about why you don't want to become a Christian and what you are afraid of, confused about, etc. Now would be a good time to ask any Christian friends you may have about it all. Or if you have not been to a good church, then now is a good time to attend. I also recommend you read <u>Broken No More: I Am Because He is</u>. Maryann's testimony has led countless people to Christ.

However, do not use this Field Manual if you are not in Christ. This would be equivalent to sending a soldier on the front lines without his gear or weapons. Once you are sure of your salvation, you may continue.

# Field Exercise 1: Deception and Lies

## Exploring Lies

This exercise fires up a lot of people with anger against the enemy. The realization that your entire life may have been dominated by lies is infuriating to so many. You may feel angry for the wasted years, the addiction, cutting, divorce, etc. When you realize your life has been impacted by lies that have crushed your dreams, your security, and self-worth for decades, you finally realize it is time to fight back! It is time to send the father of lies, Satan, back to hell where he belongs. I have watched all ages, both male and female, be verbally abused far too long by the devil's voice. The voice of Truth is the only voice we should lend ear to. I ask clients often, "Who are you sipping Starbucks with?" You know who you had coffee with based on how you feel. If you drank your latte with the enemy, you will know by your attitude and beliefs. You will feel oppressed and depressed. Your thinking will be negative, and so will your legacy. However, if you sipped a latte or cappuccino with Jesus, you might just change your destiny and bloodline.

## Field Exercise 1 Launched

### *Part 1: Replacing Lies with Truth*
Here is some space to write out the lies you have been told about yourself. Use a separate piece of paper if you run out of space. I recommend looking in a mirror. What do you see and hear?

| Lies | Truth |
|------|-------|
|  |  |
|  |  |
|  |  |
|  |  |
|  |  |

| Lies | Truth |
|------|-------|
|      |       |
|      |       |
|      |       |
|      |       |
|      |       |
|      |       |

Below are listed scriptures to replace the lies with truth. Once you complete your list of lies, speak this prayer boldly out loud to renounce the enemy's lies.

Lord Jesus, I renounce the lie that I am _____(speak all the lies on list), and I declare the truth that I am _____. (Use scriptures below.)

Shout the truth while reading the following scriptures out loud!

Note: Say these Scriptures boldly like you mean it. Soldiers fight with all they have for the glory of the God they serve. Here are examples below.

| _Truth_ | _Scripture_ |
|---------|-------------|
| ★ *I am not alone or abandoned!* | *God has said, "Never will I leave you; never will I forsake you."* *(Hebrews 13:5 NIV)* |
| ★ *I am loved and accepted and chosen!* | *"For we know, brothers and sisters[a] loved by God, that he has chosen you," (I Thessalonians 1:4 NIV)* |
| ★ *I am not helpless or hopeless!* | *"We wait in hope for the Lord;he is our help and our shield." (Psalm 33:20 NIV)* |

| | |
|---|---|
| ★ I have not been given a spirit of fear, but of power, love, and a sound mind. | For the Spirit God gave us does not make us timid, but gives us power, love and self-discipline. (2 Timothy 1:7 NIV). |
| ★ I am born of God and the evil one cannot touch me. | "We know that anyone born of God does not continue to sin; the One who was born of God keeps them safe, and the evil one cannot harm them." (1 John 5:18 NIV). |
| ★ I have been redeemed and forgiven of all my sins | "in whom we have redemption, the forgiveness of sins." (Colossians 1:14 NIV) |
| ★ I am Christ's friend. | "I no longer call you servants, because a servant does not know his master's business. Instead, I have called you friends, for everything that I learned from my Father I have made known to you. (John 15:15 NIV). |
| ★ I am a temple of God. | "Don't you know that you yourselves are God's temple and that God's Spirit dwells in your midst?" (1 Corinthians 3:16 NIV). |
| ★ I can do all things through Christ who strengthens me. | "I can do all this through him who gives me strength." (Philippians 4:13 NIV). |
| ★ I am confident that the good work Christ has begun in me will be perfected | "... being confident of this, that he who began a good work in you will carry it on to completion until the day of Christ Jesus." (Philippians 1:6 NIV). |
| ★ I have been justified. | "Therefore, since we have been justified through faith, we[a] have peace with God through our Lord Jesus Christ." (Romans 5:1 NIV). |
| ★ I have direct access to God through the Holy Spirit. | "For through him we both have access to the Father by one Spirit." (Ephesians 2:18 NIV). |

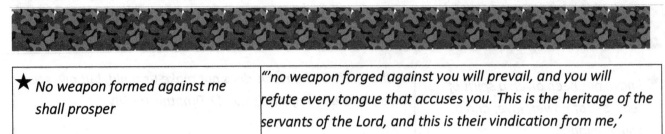

| ★ *No weapon formed against me shall prosper* | *"'no weapon forged against you will prevail, and you will refute every tongue that accuses you. This is the heritage of the servants of the Lord, and this is their vindication from me,' declares the Lord."* (Isaiah 54:17 NIV). |
|---|---|

## Part 2

When the enemy speaks to you with his lying mouth, your job is to shut it! Now look at your lies again, because I want to point out that your list of lies is really the *truth* about Satan! He is worthless, he is inadequate, he is powerless, he is ugly, his life is over, it will never get any better, the future is hopeless, and he is rejected by God!

# Field Exercise 2: Letter from God

## *Part 1*

Your assignment now is to write a letter from God to yourself. Imagine God writing to you in this moment. What would He say? This assignment allows you to hear God. Feel free to open your Bible to use the Scripture or play worship music. Too often we come into agreement with enemy's voice verses God's Word. This exercise is a sure way to replace the lies of the enemy with Truth. Again, if God were to write a letter to you, what would He say?

**Field Story Letters:** Listening to the Commander and hearing His voice is most vital on the battlefield.

## Letters from God written by Broken No More Soldiers

Below are letters inspired by the Word of God, written by clients. Names are protected for confidentiality. By faith, I believe as you read these letters that you will hear God speak directly to you. He wants you to hear Him, His Word, and not the lies. He had you in mind when He wrote them.

Don't be afraid. I am with you. You will arise from your circumstance. I have a great plan for you. Your children will not suffer like you. You will end this endless, painful cycle. You will become strong through all of this and raise your kids to be men and women of God. You are not what you are born into. Look to Me for your needs, put your faith in Me, and I will bless you. You will grow from all of this, and you will see that I've always had a great plan for you. You are not an accident but part of My plan in using you as a testimony to others. You may feel scared and weak, but with Me, nothing is impossible. This chain will end with you, and because of you, your children and generations will be blessed!

Dear Child,

You are mine. I treasure you. I love you. I desire you. I desire sweet fellowship with you. You were birthed in My heart before you were ever born in the flesh. I call you to Me, but you resist Me because you don't feel that you are worthy or that you qualify. Your sin is not so big that you cannot be cleansed. Your failings are not so severe that I can't enable and empower you. You are not so weak that you cannot be strengthened. Your secrets are not so dark that I don't see them. I know all your skeletons and I love you just the way you are. Do not allow them to come between us and keep you from the sweet fellowship with Me that I desire.

Who are you to say that you are not worthy when My Son sacrificed His life for you? Until you see yourself the way that I see you, you will not be free and I will not be glorified through you. You cannot walk in victory until you embrace the truth of how valued and precious you are to Me. Trust Me, son.

I lovingly and carefully created you. I designed you with a perfect, intentional plan for your life. Only when you collaborate with Me in using your divinely bestowed personality, gifting, and talents will you reach the deep satisfaction you desire and I will receive the glory that is Mine.

You think that you trust Me, but your worry-filled, negative words betray you. I am your all-sufficient provider, and I have demonstrated that to you when all logic, mathematical calculations, and common sense would say otherwise.

Do not be discouraged when people fail to listen to you, understand you, encourage you, value you, or honor you. I do, and I always will. I hear your voice all the time, whether you are complaining or praising. I get you like nobody else. I encourage you through My Word. Trust Me to meet you in it as you read it.

My arms are always open to embrace you. Let Me give you the kind of hug that matters—the one you need, the one you long for, the one that draws you to My heart.

I love you endlessly and unconditionally, Your Heavenly Father

My dearly beloved Daughter,

I have been with you when you struggled as a child, as you forgave your dad and mom. You have no reason to feel like a failure. I love you no matter what. You know I love you, because you have a compassion/caring heart. Even when you could be angry, I am beside you when you feel betrayed by family and friends. I love you even when you think you are to blame for your children's life choices. I love you when you blame yourself for your failed marriage and finances. But trust Me: I have a plan for you. Continue to have faith in Me. Love Me like I love you, and never stop being who you are!

I love you.

God

## Field Exercise 2 Launched

Now that you have read God's letters, it is your turn to sit with God and allow Him through the Holy Spirit to speak to you in a letter. In the space provided below, or on separate paper, let God write to you. He will speak truth that will encourage you and assist in your freedom. Please keep this letter in a safe place, as you will revisit later.

If you need help getting started, try writing, "To my dearly beloved son/daughter/child," or maybe just "John/Mary/Susie," and see where God takes it.

_____

_____

_____

_____

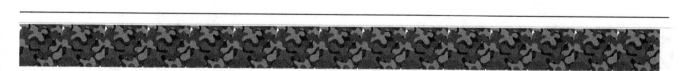

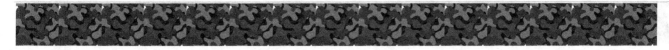

### *The Power of Speaking Letters*

Do you remember in the very beginning of this Boot Camp Field Manual that I mentioned completing these exercises out loud? Well, it is time to declare the words in your letter out loud. This is the greatest way to replace the enemy's lies you have believed far too long.

What would happen, soldier, if you truly believed your letter from God? What would happen if you believed the truth of what the Word says about you? What would happen if we all believed God's voice over the enemy's? How about less death on the battlefield? Fewer suicides? Less divorce? Murder? Jealousy? Abortion? Adultery, Addiction? Cutting? Sexual Immorality? Fewer people in mental wards and less depression? Less anxiety? Fewer graveyards filled? No more defeat!

# Field Exercise 3: Forgiveness

## Forgiveness

This may be the most powerful of all steps in this Field Manual (apart from salvation). Forgiveness is a vital act of obedience for your healing. You must forgive to set the captive free; the captive is *you*, not the offender!

The Bible says we must submit to God first then resist the enemy and he will flee from you (James 4:7 NIV). A spirit of unforgiveness means you are not submitting to God, which further means you cannot resist the devil. The Word also states in *Matthew 6:15 (NIV), "But if you do not forgive others their sins, your father will not forgive your sins."* When we choose not to forgive an offense, we give that person permission to control us, thus being our master. This permits the enemy to hold a demonic power over you, furthermore preventing you from freedom and the ability to war and win against Satan.

What power do you have, soldier, if your prayers are hindered? How can you pray and intercede on behalf of others if you are chained to unforgiveness? Chances are the very person who hurt you is the same person that needs the power of your prayers to help set them free. By the way, if your offender is a nonbeliever, you are held to a greater standard by God as you are in Christ, no longer blind, deaf, and dumb. You hold the keys to heaven, and they are probably holding the keys to hell. They are powerless against Satan, whereas you hold tremendous power in Christ to defeat him. *Isaiah 59:2 (NIV)* states, *"But your iniquities have separated you from your God; your sins have hidden his face from you, so that he will not hear."*

The Lord also commands us to love others as He has loved us. I ask you this: what is one of the greatest acts of love that Christ represents? The answer is the forgiveness of sins. What the Lord commands in Scripture is not optional, and loving others as He has loved us means to forgive your offender. The offender may not deserve forgiveness, but neither did you for your sins. Forgiving means obeying Jesus, not Satan, thus submitting to God and not the enemy. Is this a difficult step? Absolutely! But the

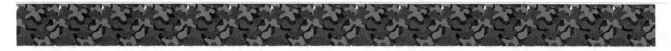

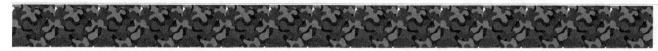

freedom is a far greater experience than holding on to bitterness and resentment with a powerless prayer life and a life of defeat.

What does forgiveness look like on the battlefield?

Imagine you are on the front lines and you just witnessed an attack on one of your most valiant men. You have all the knowledge and skills necessary to rescue him; you know he needs to be carried off the field. However, the enemy is hovering over him and getting ready to go in for the kill. His plan is to destroy him. The soldier that is down is hopeless and sees only defeat and death. Yet in all his fear, he sees you, and with his last ounce of hope, he calls on you for help. You, in all the training and skill, know how to save his life and fight the enemy from taking this soldier's last breath. Without question, you run to his rescue, knowing you have the power to overcome the enemy and rescue the dying. On the battlefield, you are now face-to-face with the enemy, yet when you go to draw your sword, you realize you are chained around the arms. You try with all your might to fight the enemy, yet you can't. Your chains are too strong and too heavy. You are chained to bitterness, resentment, hate, anger, sadness, slander, and vengeance. The sword you had trusted to rescue you is now the enemy's sword. You, through the spirit of unforgiveness, have given your sword to Satan and permitted him to chain you. Now, on the field, you are hopeless.

How can you rescue the wounded when you yourself are chained? This is what unforgiveness looks like in the spiritual battle field. Unfortunately, it is a sin that has conquered many! Let your forgiveness chain you to a sword—not Satan.

### *Field Story*

A client walked into my office years ago chained in the area of unforgiveness. Her son was molested by a family member. Her anger and sense of guilt for not protecting her son controlled her. "How can you forgive a pedophile?" she asked. "How can I forgive myself?"

As a mom, I have to be honest: the flesh rose up in me wanting to speak harshly against this man and the act. I questioned if I could forgive in the same circumstance. In fact, I felt in that moment that the perpetrator did not deserve forgiveness. I was angry. As she was weeping, I began to pray silently. "Lord, only you have the answer to this broken

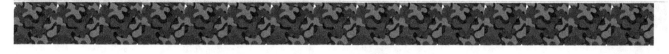

woman regarding her son. Please give me your wisdom, as I know she needs to break this chain of unforgiveness. But how?"

Instantly I heard God say in my spirit, "Vengeance is mine, and that little one belongs to me." I also heard Matt 18:6. "If anyone causes one of these little ones who trust in me to stumble, it would be better for them to have a large millstone hung around their neck and to be drowned in the depths of the sea." In that moment, I felt God's anger for such acts. I shared the Scriptures God gave me and conveyed to this mom that forgiving this man meant that she would get out of the way of God. If she did not forgive, she would continue to hold on to an act she had no power to change. However, if she were to forgive, that act would be handed over to the God of change, the God of healing, the God who says, "Vengeance is Mine."

I said to my client, "I know you may want to watch when He seeks vengeance regarding sexual assault on a child, but He died for that pedophile and that makes the offender more of God's business than your business, as you did not die for the pedophile. Your son that was molested is God's son. Furthermore, you will always be chained to the molester, and so will your son, if you don't forgive. Your son needs to break free from the spiritual chain, and as a mother in Christ, you have the power to break that chain connecting the three of you: you, your son, and the offender. When you forgive, your son will be chained to Jesus! You decide."

This mom made the most courageous and powerful decision of her life. She forgave and set her son free. She forgave herself and was freed! As she and I wept together, there was no denying the presence of God in that office. All I could speak through my tears was "Well done, good and faithful servant. Well done." She and her son are free!

## Field Exercise 3 Launched
In order to complete this next field exercise, please ask God to reveal to your mind those that have hurt you.

"NO SOLDIER LEFT BEHIND"

Please say the following prayer out loud:

*Dear Jesus, please reveal to my mind every act of offense that has been committed against me. I confess that I have not forgiven others as you have forgiven me. I have wanted to seek vengeance. I ask you, dear Lord, to forgive me. Please set me free from the bondage of my unforgiveness in order that I would be set free and no longer be controlled by my sinful nature. Lord, I choose to submit to You. Thank You, Jesus, for the healing and freedom I am about to receive as You reveal these areas of unforgiveness. In Jesus' Name, amen.*

Make a list of people that have offended you. Do not overlook forgiving yourself and, when needed, God. Obviously, we are not in any position to forgive God. But when you have thoughts that rise up against God, it clearly shows there is an offense with Him. He knows your heart, so you can't hide your feelings toward Him. I recommend you add Him to your list and allow Him to gently heal you in His love, not condemnation. You need three columns to complete this exercise. In column 1, name the offender, in column 2 write what they did, and in column 3, state how it made you feel.

| Offender's Name | What the Offender Did? | How It Made You Feel? |
|---|---|---|
| | | |
| | | |
| | | |
| | | |
| | | |
| | | |
| | | |
| | | |
| | | |
| | | |
| | | |
| | | |
| | | |
| | | |
| | | |
| | | |

| | | |
|---|---|---|
| | | |
| | | |
| | | |
| | | |

Note: Unforgiveness can get you killed on the battlefield. (If you are chained from head to foot, you can't wield your sword to take down the enemy.)

Forgive from your heart. (Bring those damaged emotions to the surface.)

Forgiveness is your choice; no one can make you do it.

For each offender, please say this prayer out loud:

*Lord Jesus, I choose on this day to forgive_____ (name of person) for _____(offense listed here) because it made me feel _____ (Share your pain. I felt abandoned, betrayed, disrespected, unloved, unwanted, ashamed, guilty, dirty, worthless, ugly …).*

After you have forgiven every person and the painful experience, please pray this following statement out loud:

*Forgiving others:*
*Lord Jesus, forgive them, Father, for they know not what they do. I choose to forgive my offenders as You have forgiven me. I renounce my right to hold on to my bitterness and resentment, and I ask You to free me from my painful emotions. Set me free from my chains of bondage. I ask you, Lord, to bless those that have offended me. Set _____(name) free, Lord. In Jesus' Name.*

*Forgiving self:*
*Lord Jesus, I choose to forgive myself for _____(list how you have hurt yourself. It may be addiction, self-harm, adultery…) because it made me feel (worthless, ashamed, guilty, alone, abandoned…) I choose not to hold on to by bitterness and self-hate. Forgive me Jesus for not forgiving myself and receiving Your grace by the blood shed for me on that cross. I now ask You to bless me and set me free. In Jesus' Name.*

"NO SOLDIER
LEFT BEHIND"

*Forgiving God:*

*Lord Jesus, I confess that I have had thoughts of blame and anger rise up against You. I have questioned your integrity and blamed you for _____ (list your offenses with God). These offenses have made me feel (abandoned, unloved, worthless, unseen, etc.). I choose today to trust You and your plan for my life. I release these thoughts against You. You are a trustworthy God and I now thank You for my pain as I trust you to use it for good. In Jesus' Name.*

After forgiving your offenders, I challenge you to go further to assist in your healing. This next exercise is not for the weak but for the strong. Do this in your quiet time with God.

I ask that you write a forgiveness letter from God to your offender. I am not suggesting you share this with your offender. I am simply asking you do this so you can remove yourself as the victim and see your offender as God sees them. This is the most challenging yet most freeing assignment for any soldier on the field. This ensures your freedom! This ensures your victory on the battlefield. *Once you complete your letters, share them with a highly respected soldier you can trust.* Or at least share with God.

_____

_____

_____

_____

_____

_____

_____

_____

_____

_____

_____

_____

_____

_____

_____

_____

_____

_____

_____

_____

_____

_____

_____

_____

_____

_____

_____

_____

# Field Exercise 4: Bury the Dead

## Bury the Dead

It is time to bury the dead! Sometimes we need to literally bury things in our lives that have died. What in your life needs to go into the ground for good? This is a field exercise that has assisted many to let go of the things that have been too much weight. Understand this: burying the dead means taking it out of your own hands and placing the dead in God's hands. What do you mean, Maryann? This is crazy! I know, right? I ask you again, "What has died in your life? Your marriage? A relationship? A dream? Your health? Or what do you need to give to God? Depression, addiction, or fear?? What needs to be resurrected? Did your marriage die and you want it resurrected? Did a dream die that needs to come back to life? Are your finances dead?

The Bible is clear that there is but one man that conquered death, and one man that conquered the grave. Jesus was resurrected from the dead. Jesus Christ knows how to resurrect the dead! For example, burying the dead is not literally placing your husband in the ground because your marriage has died. It means placing your pain in God's hands, knowing that when you bury your marriage because it seems to have died and there is no life left, you believe He will resurrect that marriage.

By faith, you bury the marriage into the ground, pray over it, and leave it there. Have your final words with God. But once it is buried, don't dig it back up. If you bury fear, believe God will bring peace and courage to life. If you bury a dream, believe God will resurrect a better one! Are you with me? Good! Time to go for a march. Literally we are going to open the ground up and place the dead there.

### *Field Story*

A woman during a Boot Camp buried her relationship with her son. We as a group walked to a creek. She left the group for a long time to bury several rocks. She knew she had to trust God for His salvation and for the restoration of a relationship. After she prayed over what she buried, she stood up knowing she will never revisit her worry again. She turned it over to God for a mighty resurrection. What she did not know was how soon God

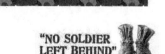

would answer her prayers by bringing back to life a relationship that had been dead far too long. The Boot Camp ended on a Sunday. What this mom did not know was that God had already begun a work in her son. In less than a week, she and her son were communicating again. She began to share with him about the retreat and her faith. His response was that he could not understand what was happening to him but that he desired to know more about God! The Bible says, *"He sets apart the godly for himself and he will hear us when we call." (Psalm 4:3 NIV)!* Can you scream hoorah? This woman's prayers were heard!

## Field Exercise 4 Launched

Now go! Grab an instrument to dig with. Take a walk and find that perfect place where you can finally let it go. I recommend grabbing some rocks and a permanent marker. On each rock, write what you are burying: fear, love, worthlessness, a relationship with a child, your husband's salvation, wife's depression, bulimia, cutting, sexual immorality, etc. Bury the dead!

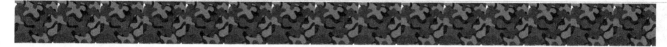

# Field Exercise 5: Thanking God

Thanking God even when you don't feel like it is an act of faith. The last thing the enemy wants you to understand is that there is power in gratitude! Thanking God for life's trials is a sure act of putting your circumstance in perspective and proves your trust in Him. Your faith in thanking Him unleashes the supernatural hand of God to move on your behalf and heal you from bitterness, resentment, unforgiveness, etc. Either you are going to thank God or be bitter toward Him. Thanking Him propels us from devastation to destiny.

When I think of the apostle Paul, I know he was thankful for being thrown into prison and for his beatings and shackles. He faced death constantly. Yet even while in prison, beaten, battered, and bruised, he began to praise God with a song. That's called gratitude, faith, and trust! He faced death; yet still sang. What happens next in the scripture supports this field exercise and the power thereof. The Bible states that while Paul was praising God, a mighty earthquake took place, his shackles were broken, and all the captives were set free. Imagine that! He thanked God with song and bam! The supernatural hand of God set him free from his chains. The Bible states in *Acts 16:26 (NIV)*, *"Suddenly there was such a violent earthquake that the foundations of the prison were shaken. At once all the prison doors flew open, and everyone's chains came loose."*

Oh, but wait! It did not end before the guard who was in charge of him attempted suicide for the responsibility and release of criminals. The Bible states, "The jailer woke up, and when he saw the prison doors open, he drew his sword and was about to kill himself because he thought the prisoners had escaped." *Acts 16:27 (NIV).* He knew he was doomed for losing the prisoners. However, Paul stopped the guard immediately and shouted, *in verses 28-30, "Don't harm yourself! We are all here!" The jailer called for lights, rushed in and fell trembling before Paul and Silas. He then brought them out and asked, "Sirs, what must I do to be saved?"*
*"*

In that God moment, the guard became a follower of Christ. Why? I believe the guard felt the atmosphere of worship and gratitude. God's presence was invited through gratitude, and He showed up. The guard could not figure out how Paul could offer such praise and gratitude to a God who permitted imprisonment, beatings, and nearly death. When we thank God through worship, not only will our chains break, but "guards" will find themselves wanting to worship too! Thus many are set free! We see this right here …

The guard took Paul home where he tended his wounds, and before nightfall, the guard's entire family became followers of Christ. *"At that hour of the night the jailer took them and washed their wounds; then immediately he and all his household were baptized." Acts 16:33 (NIV)*. This is the power of thankful worship! Not only does your gratitude move God, but it also moves others to see God.

### *Field Story*

I never fully understood the power of gratitude until I was challenged directly from God to thank Him for a loved one's deployment to Afghanistan. Let me pause for a moment to recognize our military. If you are a military spouse, first I would like to thank you for leading your family through many unknown days and nights. If you are a military member or a veteran, thank you for our freedom and the sacrifices you have made for our country to be the greatest nation in the world. Thank you!

I share this story now as former spouse of an active-duty service member. It was a hot summer day where the children and I said our farewells for the next six months. Mike deployed late June right before our nation's Fourth of July. My first Sunday at church was the hardest, as I would sit with Mike every Sunday to listen to my pastor preach and praise God during the worship. This Sunday was vastly different. My heart was heavy, and I was riddled with fear and bitterness. As a counselor, you want to be able to comfort all, but I did not have it in me, as I could not even comfort or counsel my kids who were in despair over their dad's deployment. I lay in bed that evening while holding two children as they wept in confusion over their dad's deployment. I did too, but in secret. Questions that night were hard to answer. "Mom, is Dad going to be okay?" "Mom, can Dad get killed out there?" "Mom, why did God send Dad?" "Mom, will he die out there?"

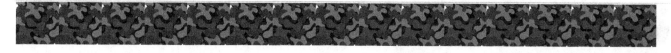

You can imagine how hopeless I felt not being able to comfort their pain. Their hearts were broken and confused. Honestly, I was a bit hurt that God sent him. I tried pulling the Christian counselor card on Him with "Hey God, I've been pouring into broken marriages watching them be healed by your hand; why my marriage hardship? I've helped countless sheep on your behalf." I know it was selfish and stupid of me, but I am just being honest. So there we were at church. I sat in the back to feel sorry for myself. I had already decided I was not going to sing those "God bless America" songs! I thought it must be easy for these church people to praise the Lord and sing. After all, their husbands are not deployed to a war zone where our soldiers are dying daily. I will sit here, Lord, in church, but I will not sing.

As you can imagine, God did not let me get away with such a plan. I believe He saw how pitiful I was and decided to intervene! As I stood listening to the worship lyrics, I began to hear His still, small voice. I felt as though He was saying He wanted me to sing and worship Him. As though I needed to praise Him rather than be hurt. I started thinking that six months of my poor attitude was only going to give the devil gratitude and power. In my mind I heard, "Maryann, I thought you of all people, with your counseling and armor of God would know better." Well, one thing I did know was that I knew better than to argue with God! So I began to sing at His request. I felt as though He asked me to praise louder! I thought *Really, Lord? You are pushing it!* But I obeyed. I began to sing, and as I sang, I began to feel Him. I began to trust Him. I began to sing with all my heart, because the more I sang, the more I felt the power of His presence. Before I knew it, He wrapped me in His arms in the back of that church. My hands that I refused to raise in worship were stretched out as far as I could reach. I wanted to touch heaven. In that moment, my fear vanished, as did my resentment and bitterness. I was in His arms, and I was going to be okay! In fact, I felt a courage release in me to accomplish a six-month mission and assignment from God.

As the music was ending, it felt as though He asked, "Maryann, do you trust Me?" It was not an audible voice, just a feeling. I said, "Yes, Lord, of course I do!" It was then that I felt Him ask me to thank Him for deploying Mike. I knew this would be a great act of obedience!

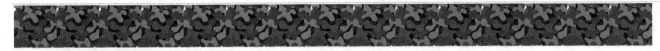

I closed my eyes and felt the warmth of God's love for me, and before I knew it, I was speaking, "Thank You for sending Mike." I felt prompted to speak again, only louder and confident. "Thank You, God, for sending Mike!" After speaking those words out of obedience, I felt as though no one was even in that church. I was in a realm far removed from all the voices. It was as though it was just Him and me. I wept with God and felt so free from the unknowns about Mike's deployment. Nothing else mattered. As the worship ended, I felt as though God had one last request. Just one more question for me regarding thanking Him. He wanted to know if I trusted Him. I felt as though to prove my trust, He was asking me to thank Him even if Mike did not return home. This was the ultimate test! However, when you are in the presence of the Almighty and wrapped in His love, that love dispels all human reasoning and fear. You do what He says! And so I thanked Him out loud with tears streaming. I opened my mouth with such trust and gratitude. "Thank You, God! Even if he does not return, I thank You!" No longer was I carrying Mike and our family; I left with God carrying us.

I would like to share now the supernatural power that was released that day. Six months later, Mike did return, but he returned with his own God story. The same day I was thanking God at my church, he was flown into a FOB (forward operating base) that had an unenviable reputation for receiving very heavy attacks from the Taliban. The Taliban, knowing that the Fourth of July is the United States' Independence Day, seemed to enjoy adding their own version of fireworks in the form of mortar and rocket attacks on the US outpost. Mike was told that for the past ten years, the Fourth of July was a dangerous day to be in this FOB and that everyone was to get ready for the barrage. On the night of the third, as he lay in his bunk waiting and praying, he asked God to care for his family if he did not return.

As he was praying, he suddenly felt God's presence like never before. It was as though God was in the room with him, by his bedside. Mike was moved to tears as he felt the same warmth I too had felt in church. He was at peace knowing God was trustworthy. Just as God was about to leave Mike's bedside, Mike wholeheartedly said, "No, don't leave me, Lord" to which the Holy One engulfed him yet again with His presence.

"NO SOLDIER LEFT BEHIND"

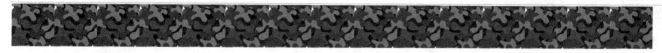

Miraculously, that night came and went with no attacks. The next day, the Fourth of July, also came and went. Everyone was required to wear all of their body armor (flak vests and helmets), not taking off any of the gear even while inside the chow tent or other semi protected areas. The next several days were the same: nothing! Not one rocket! Not one attack. In ten years this area had been rocketed by the Taliban, yet the year Mike lay in his bed, and the same day I thanked God for sending Mike, even if he did not return, was the year that not one rocket or missile was launched!

A few days later, Mike was flown out of that FOB to go farther south in the country. I believe thanking God unleashed His supernatural hand to heal me and protect Mike and us. God is faithful and deserves our thanksgiving, even when it doesn't make sense. Your healing is on the other side!

Months later Mike received word that a devastating attack was executed by the Taliban on that very FOB, with the main wall penetrated and many fatalities reported in an area very close to where Mike slept.

## Field Exercise 5 Launched

You need a paper, pen, snot rags, and an empty chair. Imagine Christ, your Savior, sitting in that chair. I want you to *write a letter to Him for all the things you have never thanked Him for.* Just like Paul, thank Him and praise Him for your circumstance, and thank Him for the injuries. Chances are your hardships in life are what drew you near to Him. Thanking Him means we no longer question God's integrity. My devastation brought me to salvation, and I thank Him for all the pain. It has made me a better soldier and counselor. God has used my story to bring many into the kingdom. My devastation was worth it! What about you?

_____

_____

_____

_____

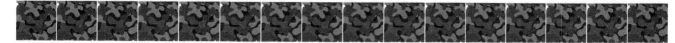

# Field Exercise 6: War Box

## War Box

Now that you have completed all five of the previous field exercises, it is time to make a war box. A war box is a box that contains Scripture from the Word of God and your previous letters. I recommend using this box daily. Speak the Word over your home, life, and family. Reread your letters as a reminder of your field experience with your commander, God. I recommend placing this box in a room where you feel most oppression or hear those nagging thoughts. Below is a powerful field story about a battle that was overcome by use of the war box.

## *Field Story*

I once had a client that was addicted to lustful actions. As a Christian counselor, I knew the power of the Word when read, meditated on, and spoken out loud. This client would also have nightmares and struggled with pornography. After she completed her war box, I asked her to place the box in the room in which she was most tempted with sexual vulnerability. She placed this war box in her bedroom. Every night, she would open up her war box and in the midst of great temptation speak the Word out loud. She was amazed to see that she was walking in victory and not defeat. She had learned her authority in Christ. She had a sword (the Word) and began to raise it! Her testimony is now a testimony of freedom and purity! This is one of many countless war box stories! You may make as many boxes as you wish! The point of this assignment is to use your God-given weapons (your mouth and the Word) and take back territory. Satan must flee when you declare His Word!

"NO SOLDIER LEFT BEHIND"

## Field War Box Exercise 6 Launched

Start worship music and have it playing in the background while writing scriptures on index cards. Place your war words in your war box (any container).

The point of this exercise is to speak the Scriptures when feeling oppressed. Below are some recommended Scriptures for war boxes. You may choose ten or so for your box. Choose the Scripture that suits your battle call best!

Some Recommended Scriptures:

★ "Greater is He that is in me than he that is in this world!" *"You, dear children, are from God and have overcome them, because the one who is in you is greater than the one who is in the world. (1 John 4:4 NIV).*

★ I have all authority and power to tread on serpents and scorpions and over all the power of the enemy, and nothing shall injure me! *"I have given you authority to trample on snakes and scorpions and to overcome all the power of the enemy; nothing will harm you." (Luke 10:19 NIV).*

★ I have the power and authority over all demons and sickness. *"When Jesus had called the Twelve together, he gave them power and authority to drive out all demons and to cure diseases," (Luke 9:1 NIV).*

★ In the name of Jesus Christ, I command Satan to flee from me. My mind and body are healed by his power. *"Calling the Twelve to him, he began to send them out two by two and gave them authority over impure spirits... They drove out many demons and anointed many sick people with oil and healed them." (Mark 6:7–13 NIV).*

★ No weapon formed against me or my family shall prosper! *" no weapon forged against you will prevail, and you will refute every tongue that accuses you. This is the heritage of the servants of the Lord, and this is their vindication from me," declares the Lord. (Isaiah 54:17 NIV),*

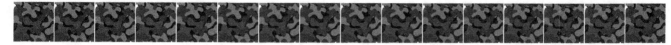

★ *"Through you we push back our enemies; through your name we trample our foes.
I put no trust in my bow, my sword does not bring me victory; but you give us victory over our enemies, you put our adversaries to shame. In God we make our boast all day long, and we will praise your name forever." (Psalm 44:5-8 NIV).*

★ *"For the eyes of the Lord range throughout the earth to strengthen those whose hearts are fully committed to him." (2 Chronicles 16:9 NIV).*

★ *"With flattery he will corrupt those who have violated the covenant, but the people who know their God will firmly resist him." (Daniel 11:32).*

★ *"This is the word of the Lord to Zerubbabel: 'Not by might nor by power, but by my Spirit,' says the Lord Almighty." (Zechariah 4:6 NIV).*

★ *"As for you, the anointing you received from him remains in you." (1 John 2:27 NIV).*

★ *"But you have an anointing from the Holy One, and all of you know the truth." (1 John 2:20 NIV).*

★ *"No one will be able to stand against you all the days of your life. As I was with Moses, so I will be with you; I will never leave you nor forsake you. ⁶ Be strong and courageous," (Joshua 1:5 NIV).*

★ *"Praise be to the Lord my Rock, who trains my hands for war, my fingers for battle.
He is my loving God and my fortress, my stronghold and my deliverer, my shield, in whom I take refuge, who subdues peoples under me." (Psalm 144:1-2 NIV).*

★ *"You, Lord, are my lamp; the Lord turns my darkness into light. With your help I can advance against a troop; with my God I can scale a wall. "As for God, his way is perfect: The Lord's word is flawless; he shields all who take refuge in him." (2 Samuel 22:29-31 NIV).*

★ *"It is God who arms me with strength and keeps my way secure. He makes my feet like the feet of a deer; he causes me to stand on the heights. He trains my hands for battle; my arms can bend a bow of bronze. You make your saving help my shield, and your right hand sustains me; your help has made me great. You provide a broad path for my feet, so that my ankles do not give way. I pursued my enemies and overtook them; I did not turn back till they were destroyed. I crushed them so that they could not rise; they fell beneath my feet. You armed me with strength for battle; you humbled my adversaries before me." (Psalm 18:32-39 NIV).*

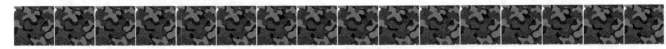

★ *"The Lord is my rock, my fortress and my deliverer; my God is my rock, in whom I take refuge, my shield and the horn of my salvation. He is my stronghold, my refuge and my savior— from violent people you save me." (2 Samuel 22:2-3 NIV).*

★ *"But the Lord is faithful, and he will strengthen you and protect you from the evil one" (2 Thessalonians 3:3 NIV).*

★ *"The Lord will rescue me from every evil attack and will bring me safely to his heavenly kingdom." (2 Timothy 4:18 NIV).*

★ *"The salvation of the righteous comes from the Lord; he is their stronghold in time of trouble. The Lord helps them and delivers them; he delivers them from the wicked and saves them, because they take refuge in him." (Psalm 37:39-40 NIV).*

★ *"I lift up my eyes to the mountains— where does my help come from? My help comes from the Lord, the Maker of heaven and earth. He will not let your foot slip— he who watches over you will not slumber; indeed, he who watches over Israel will neither slumber nor sleep. The Lord watches over you— the Lord is your shade at your right hand; the sun will not harm you by day, nor the moon by night. The Lord will keep you from all harm— he will watch over your life; the Lord will watch over your coming and going both now and forevermore." (Psalm 121:1-8 NIV).*

★ *"Turn your ear to me, come quickly to my rescue; be my rock of refuge, a strong fortress to save me. Since you are my rock and my fortress, for the sake of your name lead and guide me. Keep me free from the trap that is set for me, for you are my refuge. Into your hands I commit my spirit; deliver me, Lord, my faithful God." (Psalm 31:2-5 NIV).*

★ *"The Lord is a warrior; the Lord is his name…. Your right hand, Lord, was majestic in power. Your right hand, Lord, shattered the enemy. In the greatness of your majesty you threw down those who opposed you. You unleashed your burning anger; it consumed them like stubble." (Exodus 15:3, 6-7 NIV).*

★ *"The Lord will march out like a champion, like a warrior he will stir up his zeal; with a shout he will raise the battle cry and will triumph over his enemies." (Isaiah 42:13 NIV).*

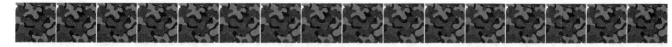

★ *"I will go before you and will level the mountains; I will break down gates of bronze and cut through bars of iron." (Isaiah 45:2 NIV).*

★ *"But you will not leave in haste or go in flight; for the Lord will go before you, the God of Israel will be your rear guard." (Isaiah 52:12 NIV).*

★ *"But be assured today that the LORD your God is the one who goes across ahead of you like a devouring fire. He will destroy them; he will subdue them before you. And you will drive them out and annihilate them quickly, as the LORD has promised you." (Deuteronomy 9:3 NIV).*

★ *"The Lord will fight for you; you need only to be still." (Exodus 14:14 NIV).*

★ *"'Be strong and courageous. Do not be afraid or discouraged because of the king of Assyria and the vast army with him, for there is a greater power with us than with him. [8] With him is only the arm of flesh, but with us is the LORD our God to help us and to fight our battles." (2 Chronicles 32:7-8 NIV).*

★ *"I will contend with those who contend with you, and your children I will save." (Isaiah 49:25 NIV).*

★ *"God is just: He will pay back trouble to those who trouble you." (2 Thessalonians 1:6 NIV).*

Place in your war box on index cards, and declare war against the enemy when you feel an attack!

You are doing great, soldier! You are almost there!

# Field Exercise 7: Spiritual House Cleansing

<u>Field House Cleansing Exercise</u>

Why do we need to cleanse our homes? I am not talking about toilets, dishes, or floors! I am talking about removing darkness. Every soldier needs a place of spiritual safety!

### *Field Story*

> Before every retreat or Boot Camp, I spiritually cleanse the house. I know that it does not take much for the enemy to enter a home that opens doors to him. I even spiritually cleanse hotel rooms before I stay in them. Imagine staying in a hotel room with your children where the former visitor watched pornography or used drugs prior to your stay. Or what if prostitution or abuse took place there? I guarantee you would want to cleanse that room! When I don't cleanse my home, often times we suffer with nightmares and/or other forms of spiritual attacks. Why would I endure that when I have the authority in Christ to command evil spirits to leave? You have a home that needs peace and God's presence. Well, Maryann, how do I do this cleaning thing? Great question! Check out the field exercise below.

### *Part 1: Field Exercise*

Which ways open the doors for the enemy in your home? And how can you keep him out?

Is there anything in the home that permits the enemy there? What do you watch on TV? What are you permitting in your house that allows demonic spirits? Is it pornography? Inappropriate music? Drugs? Tarot cards? Unforgiveness? Verbal abuse? Ask the Holy Spirit to reveal to your mind anything that must be removed for peace and protection. Once you make your list, take action! Your house needs to be a sanctuary for the Holy Spirit, not evil.

## Field Exercise 7 Launched

List of Items for Spiritual House Cleaning:

| Areas/Objects That Need To Be Cleaned Out or Removed | |
|---|---|
| | |
| | |
| | |
| | |
| | |
| | |
| | |
| | |

Renounce all open doors to the enemy by speaking this prayer:

*Lord Jesus, I turn all demonic possessions, such as _____(porn, books, movies, occult books, music, unhealthy foods that are a form of addiction, drugs, etc.), and I ask that you forgive me for permitting the enemy in my home rather than You and Your holiness. I renounce any way in which I have permitted Satan and his demons in my home by my actions, thoughts, and behavior. Forgive me for opening the door with _____, and I now ask you in the name of Jesus to cover all my sins with the blood of Jesus and cover my home, Lord, as a place of spiritual safety by Your blood. I command in the name of Jesus Christ that every evil spirit based on my activity flee! In Jesus' Name!*

Complete part 2 below in your home.

### Part 2 (Homework)

Soldier, go through your entire house with this prayer. Speak the prayer out loud and with great authority and boldness. A soldier must live and operate in a place of spiritual safety.

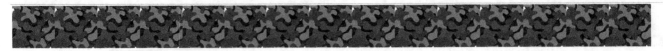

*Thank you, Jesus, for my home and place of spiritual rest, peace, and protection. Thank you that no weapon formed against me shall prosper. I declare the blood of Jesus over my home, my body, my children, and my spouse. I ask that you place Your holy angels in every corner of this room and home with their swords drawn against Satan and spiritual enemies to protect me my family and children. I declare this home to be a holy sanctuary where Your manifest presence dwells. I renounce any allegiance to Satan based on the activities from the past and present residents, visitors, and any other unknown source. I claim this room and my home to be filled with the Holy Spirit, and I command in the Name of Jesus Christ that all demonic assignments against my family, mind, health, home, pets, and all other belongings be bound in Jesus' Name. I command all evil spirits to leave this room/home and never return. I take this authority as one that has been born of God, knowing that the evil one cannot touch me! Thank you, Lord, for cleansing this home/room by Your power. Thank you for a place to sleep and rest in you. Renew my mind, Lord, and my body. Thank you for filling me with Your Holy Spirit. In Jesus' Name, amen!*

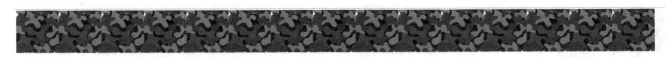

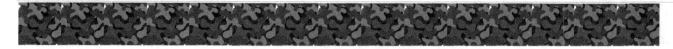

# Field Exercise 8: Sexual Sin

## Sexual Immorality

Soldier, we are about to trek on dreaded territory. However, we must take courage and complete the mission that was started. We must attack this area head on, as this is one of the most common area of assault from Satan. It is time to be free spiritually, physically, and emotionally from all sexual acts.

Let me explain.

Your body is the temple of the Holy Spirit. Christ takes residency in those that accept Christ as Lord. That means the Son of God lives in you. Satan knows this, and the very act of sexual immorality is the closest Satan can get to assaulting Christ himself! Sexual immorality is demonic, perverted, and permits spiritual strongholds to be passed onto your partner as the two become one flesh. What does that mean? It means that whatever demonic spirit that is on one person, now has permission to attach to you; thus, you are lying in a bed with legions (many)—an "orgy," if you will— Satan watches you in the very act of assaulting Christ and committing adultery in marriage to Jesus. Satan is like a sex trafficker and, dare I say, sex addict. (He tries to get in the beds of all humans to pervert sex or rob us spiritually through sex or pornography with the deception that you are not harming anyone. In using pornography or committing physical sexual immorality, the enemy then has the power to cage you and turn your temple over to perversion and more vile activities. Lust has your head, and Satan captivates your heart, leaving you staggering on the path of destruction and devastation. As a counselor, I have seen families destroyed over such acts.

### *Field Story*

A client of mine was battling with pornographic "pop-ups" since marriage. He had a history of early childhood sexual experiences, such as masturbation and pornography. Sex was very gratifying; however, once he became a believer and married under God's

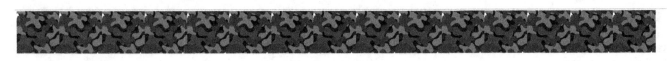

covenant, Satan began to assault sexual intimacy and the holiness of sex and began to pervert the bedroom. He could not climax without extreme perverted thoughts and/or images of pornography. Furthermore, he would have pop-ups of women that he had had prior sexual experiences with. He began to develop dread and anxiety just thinking about sex. He also began to have repulsive thoughts against his bride. However, after completing this step of renouncing and breaking free from each sexual experience, spiritually, physically, and emotionally, this man's pop-ups diminished drastically as he learned how to cast thoughts and images down and speak the Word over his bride and his marital bed. Their marriage is now free, and they were trained to recognize Satan's assaults and war with the Word.

I recommend praying together and inviting the Holy Spirit into our marriage beds, thus keeping Satan out and permitting God in. Why not kneel before your bed and invite the Holy Spirit to make you two holy, make this union of one as an act of worship presented to God rather than Satan? If this thought makes you uncomfortable, it is only because holiness in the bedroom has been hijacked by Satan. Take back the bedroom Jesus' Name!

### *Commonly Asked Questions*

- Is Masturbation a sin?

  Ask yourself these three questions first prior to answering:

  - Would you do it in front of Jesus?
  - Would you want your actions in the newspaper?
  - What are you thinking while masturbating? (Usually one fantasizes in order to climax.)

If any of the above questions make you uncomfortable, we call that conviction. If it is a conviction for you, then it is a sin for you. Paul says if it is a conviction for you, then it is a sin.

Not by coincidence, sex can be very gratifying when it is used as sin against God. The pure excitement and chemical response to sin is a great high. The brain is reprogrammed and is now vulnerable to sex addiction due to the addictive "high" you experience. Sexual sin is one of the greatest weapons the devil uses against God's children, because it is the closest he can get to assaulting Christ himself. However, once married, the sexual desire for your spouse is now under assault due to past sexual experiences. Satan uses your past as a weapon to assault a bedroom made for holiness and power. You have the power in Christ to turn a bedroom into the greatest place of worship and most beautiful moment of holy intimacy! Dare I say, "Holy sex"? If you have never experienced Holy Spirit-filled sexual intimacy, you are missing out on one of the greatest gifts God has granted us. It is never too late, regardless of your past, to claim this today in your marriage.

## Field Exercise 8 Launched

Please begin by saying the following prayer:

*Lord, Jesus, forgive me for my sin. I have allowed the enemy to use my body to glorify his kingdom rather than Your kingdom. The enemy has used my body and abused me sexually for the purpose of harming my faith, my body, my mind, my family, and future generations. I ask that You reveal all these immoral uses of my body, so that I may break free from sexual perversion, lust, and temptation. I ask that You heal me now, take my body as I commit myself to you, and make me new. Set me free, Lord. I want only to be faithful to You, Jesus. I believe that in this moment, as I speak and confess, You will break those sinful bondages. Jesus' Name, amen!*

Ask the Holy Spirit to bring to your mind all sexual immorality in your life. Include sexual immorality that was willfully done and all acts against you, such as rape, incest, sexual molestation, and masturbation. If you have questions as to why masturbation is a sin, please ask your group leader or church mentor. Next, renounce boldly out loud every experience.

If you don't remember the names of all your partners, God remembers their names. Maybe lift up the place, moment, etc.

| Name of Person or Object | Sexual Experience |
|---|---|
|  |  |
|  |  |
|  |  |
|  |  |
|  |  |
|  |  |
|  |  |
|  |  |
|  |  |
|  |  |

*Lord Jesus, I break and renounce the sexual experience _____ (name the experience, such as prostitution, oral sex, anal sex, fisting, sex texting, Skype sex, bestiality, homosexuality, perverse speaking, mental pop-ups, masturbation, emotional affairs, fantasies, swinging, and orgies) with_____ (name the person). I now renounce these acts by the authority and Name of Jesus Christ and cover these acts with the blood of Jesus, and I break that sinful bond with _____ (name the person) spiritually, physically, and emotionally.*

After you have completed your list, dedicate your new body spotless before Christ by speaking the following prayer, which is based on Galatians 3:13:

*I declare all curses over my life, through my sexual sin and lust and the sins of my ancestors, to be broken Jesus' Name. I hereby rededicate my body, mind, soul, and spirit to You, to be used for Your glory alone. I also give You my will, emotions, and affections to be controlled by Your Holy Spirit. I choose to avoid the temptations of sexual sin and to live in the Name of Jesus Christ. I command all unclean sexual spirits (lust, perversion, masturbation, pornography, etc) to leave me now. I break all unholy soul ties and ask you, Lord, to return to me all that was lost through sexual sin.*

*Forgive me God for these acts of adultery against you. I will remain pure before You and pure to my earthly marriage and in my spiritual marriage to You. Thank You for setting me free from sexual immorality. My mind and body are no longer a product of sexual immorality. I am a product of the cross and cleansed by your blood, Jesus. I reject and disown the lie that I am damaged goods and that I am not*

*acceptable to You because of my sexual sins. I believe that today I am cleansed! I am not dirty, worthless, or shameful. You, Jesus, have set me free and love and accept me just as I am. On this day, I choose to believe that I am clean in Your eyes. I am free! Jesus' Name, amen!*

## Prayers for Additional Strongholds

### *Pornography*

*Lord, I confess that I have turned to pornography to satisfy sexual lust and seek pleasure rather than seeking You for power and purity. I admit to masturbating to sexually suggestive material as a source of comfort and release rather than seeking You. Jesus, I confess that I have sinned again and again. I feel trapped in addicting habits, but I am reaching out to You in hope and faith. Thank You for dying on the cross for me. Thank You for giving me the power in the Holy Spirit to combat this area of temptation. Please forgive me and grant me a new start today. I give myself to You and invite You to be Lord of my life. Thank You for saving me from the power of sin and death. Please fill me with your Holy Spirit and give me Your power, wisdom, and grace so that I can obey you and walk according to Your ways every moment of every day. In Jesus' Name, amen!*

### *Homosexuality*

*The blood of Jesus cleanses me from all sin. I claim freedom from all sins of homosexuality that came through my eyes, ears, mind, sexual assault, confusion, or sexual activity.*

*I confess all preoccupation with sensual desires and appetites, all longing for that which is forbidden, and all unnatural affections, all unrestrained passions and lusts, and all activities that produce lewd emotions or foster sexual sin toward the same sex. I further confess all filthy communication, obscene and filthy language, course conversations and jokes, lewd and obscene music, poetry, literature, and art. I confess all forms of pornography and all acts of sodomy, adultery, immorality, fornication, masturbation, gender confusion, or homosexuality. In Jesus' Name, amen!*

# Field Exercise 9: FEAR

Fear
Soldiers don't fear the enemy; the enemy fears soldiers.

Fear is a four-letter F word on the field! And it hinders our victory. FEAR is an acronym for "false expectations appearing real." The enemy knows if we bow down to the spirit of fear, we will never have the faith to pursue our destiny. Satan wants us to fear, and a spirit of fear makes us question God's integrity. We will either fear Satan or fear God; we can't do both effectively. In fact, fear causes us to live irresponsible lives. Faith extinguishes fear, but fear will extinguish our faith. We must take courage. Courage is *not* the absence of fear; it is doing what is most fearful while afraid. Please pray and ask the Holy Spirit to reveal fears that have prevented you from moving forward for God's kingdom. What is the enemy using against you to keep you from your destiny? It is time for Satan to fear you, and you to stop fearing his lies. The surest way to defeat your fear is to do it afraid.

### *Field Story*

Renouncing fear is powerful. However, this story I am about to share takes "powerful" to another level.

It was very late after midnight when my two children ran into my room. They were just riddled with a spirit of fear. They jumped into my bed and startled me with so many fearful thoughts. Ashley, my daughter, asked if we would have an earthquake, and then my son asked if there would be a tsunami. (We live in Virginia.) The next question was regarding a tornado. Their minds were what I call hijacked with fear. It was irrational fear that made their bodies tremble. What was a mom to do? I decided to practice what I preached in a counseling session. I prayed with my children out loud and commanded the spirit of fear to leave in Jesus' Name, and then I quoted *2 Timothy 1:7 (NIV). "For the Spirit God gave us does not make us timid, but gives us power, love and self-discipline."* I then asked the kids to go back to sleep. Of course I permitted them to stay in bed with

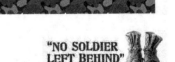
"NO SOLDIER LEFT BEHIND"

me. However, the moment I closed my eyes, I saw a pop-up of a pasty, fearful demon. I had never in my life seen a demon, and I had a hard time processing this pop-up. Of course my eyes were closed. I was very tired and could have made this up in my mind. Nonetheless, it frightened me! Now I found myself to be a bit spooked. The demon was shaking in great fear with teeth chattering. I guess it looked like a spirit of fear! Either way, I decided to speak boldly with authority and mean it! I knew there was an unseen battle, and I needed to win! So again I quoted the Scripture and demanded in Christ's Name that it leave. Instantly, peace swept through the room, and I was able to sleep, as were my kids. Praise God! This, however, does not complete my story. The next morning, Ashley and I were working on math together. She interrupted me with a statement that made chills and tears well up. She said, "Mom, last night I saw something in our room while you were sleeping. I saw the hand of God come into our room, move around our bed, and then come over the top of us!" She then said she was not scared because she knew it was the hand of God. The hand as described was huge and bright and protected us. No doubt, the Word of God is sharper than any two-edged sword. My daughter saw the supernatural happen when we rejected the fear and spoke the Word of God. Fear can only control us if we let it. This is a story that has changed my life!

## Field Exercise 9 Launched

Please state this prayer out loud: *"Lord Jesus, I ask you to reveal to my mind any spirit of fear operating in my life. God has not given me a spirit of fear but of power, love, and sound mind (2 Timothy 1–7).*

You will need paper and a pen to list your fears.

Common fears of the enemy:

- fear of abandonment
- fear of addiction
- fear of adultery

- fear of being stupid
- fear of cancer
- fear of car crash

"NO SOLDIER LEFT BEHIND"

- fear of certain people
- fear of college
- fear of committing the unpardonable sin
- fear of death
- fear of disease
- fear of divorce
- fear of driving
- fear of failure
- fear of fear
- fear of financial failure
- fear of flying
- fear of germs

- fear of going crazy
- fear of having a heart attack
- fear of heights
- fear of homosexuality
- fear of marriage
- fear of never being loved
- fear of not getting married
- fear of public speaking
- fear of rejection
- fear of Satan
- fear of forgiving
- fear of worthlessness

List all of your fears:

| My Fears ||
|---|---|
|  |  |
|  |  |
|  |  |
|  |  |
|  |  |
|  |  |
|  |  |
|  |  |

State the below prayer out loud to renounce the power of fear over your life.

*Lord Jesus, I choose to renounce _____(list your fears), and I choose to fear You alone. God, You have not given me a spirit of fear but of powerful love and sound mind. I claim the sound mind of Christ and ask for the renewal of my mind. Thank You for conquering my fears, Lord, as Your love casts out all fear. May I go unafraid and trust in you. I command Satan to leave, in the name of Jesus Christ, and I command the spirit of fear to leave my presence! Forgive me, Lord, for questioning You and not trusting You to care for me. Thank You for setting me free! In Jesus' Name.*

Note: Satan will tempt you to fear; he will not stop. You must maintain your freedom during attack. Remember your war box! Use it!

# Field Exercise 10: Letter from God to Another Soldier

I challenge you to be inspired by the Holy Spirit to write a letter from God to an individual God places on your heart during this Broken No More Boot Camp, counseling session or small group. You could change a life, change a relationship, and mend brokenness. Essentially, this is your opportunity to war on behalf of someone that is in captivity. This letter will be written with great power, as you are walking in greater freedom than ever before. Why not continue this after your Boot Camp weekend or small group? What if you handed a letter to a grocery store bagger? Starbucks barista? Your child? An estranged family member? Of course, the Holy Spirit must lead you. This will bring to you such great joy and to God great joy! This exercise brings deep healing and increases believers' courage on the field.

Dear Faith,

I want you to know how proud I am of you and of how far you have come in your walk of faith in Me. You have been through much hurt and disappointment in your life that the enemy used to cause you despair and tried to destroy you with. You have experienced much difficulty and sorrow in your past and have learned firsthand that in this world you will experience trouble, but that is not the end of the story. I have overcome the world. People will sometimes let you down but even then I want you to remember that I am always present with you.

You have been open to My Spirit and My instruction and that has brought you to a life of freedom. Learn from the past but never live there. You are never ever alone and I will never let you down or leave or forsake you. You must remember this truth and hold on to it. Every day I want you to live in My presence. Continue to practice acknowledging My presence throughout each day.

Your life is a journey of discovering who you are in Me and what I want you to do. I want you to continue to walk in the freedom you have discovered for the rest of your life. You are on the right path to a deeper understanding of Who I Am. I will continue to reveal more and more of Myself to you. I have so much more love and joy ahead for you! I have great plans ahead for you! What the enemy has

meant for evil to destroy you, I am going to use not only for your good but for the good of others. I work all things together for the good of those who love Me and are called according to My purposes. As you continue to walk in my purposes you will see how I will use you as an instrument of My love and grace in the lives of others who have been attacked and lied to by the enemy. I am going to use you to show the same compassion and love to others that I have shown to you. You must always remember to keep your Armor on. Stay in My Word and declare My Word over your life. My Word and My Spirit set you free and will keep you free! I am what you need and always will be. Remember not to seek what you need in anything or anyone else as it will never be enough. I want you to continue to experience the depths and heights of My love! My love will sustain you! My love will propel you to new heights in Me. Your future is bright and beautiful!!

I love you and cherish you my daughter,

Your Heavenly Father

## Field Exercise 10: Launched

Hand your letter with great boldness to the person He directed you to. Intense blessing is just around the corner! If at a Boot Camp or in a small group, I recommend you read this letter out loud to a group member. There is power when we declare His Word over others! That is what soldiers do!

# Field Exercise 11: Generational Sin

## Generational Sin

The Bible states that the iniquities of one generation can be visited on the third and fourth generations, but God's blessings will be poured out on a thousand generations for those who love and obey Him (Exodus 20:4–6). God's promise cannot be revoked! All of the pain and sins from our past does not have to impact our future, our children, or generations to come. We can choose to ask God to release us by repenting and asking God to forgive us. I would add your family name, maiden name, and all the last names of your ancestors as far back as you can remember. You are not at fault for their sins, but these sins can and have influenced you regardless.

## Field Exercise 11 Launched

*Lord Jesus Christ, please bring to my mind all the generational sins in my bloodline that have harmed me, held me in bondage, and influenced me negatively. Since I am now in Christ, I want to maintain my freedom and walk in my new identity as a product of the cross, not a product of my past or family sins. I want to experience my freedom. In Jesus' Name, amen.*

Use this checklist to write down generational sin:

- abandonment
- abortion
- abuse (emotional, physical, mental, sexual)
- addictions
- adultery

- anger, rage, violence
- bearing false witness (lying to defend yourself or others)
- cancers
- control, possessiveness, manipulation
- coveting (wanting what others have)

- criticism
- disease
- divorce
- drunkenness
- eating disorder
- emotional dependency
- false religions
- fears (all kinds)
- gambling
- gluttony
- gossip
- greed/materialism
- homosexuality
- idolatry (false gods, money, food drugs, sex)
- incest
- jealousy
- laziness
- lying
- man gods (men being your master, not God)
- masturbation
- miscarriages
- molestation
- murder (hate,  seeking vengeance)
- nightmares
- not caring for children
- not honoring my mother or father
- not honoring the Sabbath rest (A command to rest is not an option, workaholic.)
- occult practices _____(Name them.)
- parents and children exchange roles
- perfectionism
- physical infirmities
- pride
- racism
- rape
- rebellion
- rejection, insecurity
- religious bondage, cults
- Satanism, witchcraft,
- Self-mutilation
- sexual dysfunction
- sexual sin and perversion
- stealing
- suicide
- television, music, books, or games that were ungodly
- unbelief
- unforgiveness
- unworthiness, low self-esteem, inferiority
- using the Lord's name in vain (swearing)
- women gods (women being your master, not God

  _____
- OTHERS_____

### Field Story

As a child of God, I renounced my generational strongholds. Nearly all of the above were curses on my generation. But today I am free! I watched a family member renounce

alcoholism and literally saw her face transform as she was released from this stronghold. I have been sober for sixteen years. I believe I broke this horrible curse of addiction. No longer will I pass down baggage to my generations. I will pass down blessings!

**For Boot Camp attendees and small groups, we will approach the cross as one army to shout our declaration of freedom over our generations. I encourage you to pull up a picture from your smartphone of family, a child, etc. and lay them at the foot of the cross.**

Now begin to write your bloodline sins. After you have written all the generational sins, please add the family names of your ancestors, including maiden names. After you complete the writing exercise, renounce all the sin as follows out loud.

| Generational/ Bloodline Sins | |
|---|---|
| | |
| | |
| | |
| | |
| | |
| | |
| | |
| | |
| | |

Declare!

*Lord, I renounce_____ (list the sins in your bloodline).*

*Thank You for setting me free. I reject and disown any spoken curse or action over me and my family. I declare that Christ has restored my bloodline. I renounce all satanic assignments directed against me, my family, my children, and my marriage, and I command Satan in the Name of Jesus Christ to go to back to the bottomless pit where he belongs! I declare my family to be free and claim my spiritual heritage in Christ! From this day forward, I release the blessings and accept God's Word over me and my family. We are seated with Christ in the heavenly realm, our names are written in the Lamb's book of life, and my*

*family and I will serve in God's army and fulfill the destiny God has set before us. My bloodline is free from condemnation. It cannot be separated from God's love. My bloodline is established, appointed, and sealed by God. I am born of God and the evil one cannot touch me or my family! I now submit to God and resist the enemy and I command every spiritual and demonic spirit to leave my presence and generations to come and to never return. I put on the full Armor of God! I declare the helmet of salvation, the breastplate of righteousness, the Sword of the Spirit, the belt of truth, and the shoes that bring forth the good news as my family's armor! From this day forward, I will stand against Satan's' lies, temptations, and deceptions. I declare my family under the blood of Jesus. It is finished!*

Please note additional prayers that you may need to speak to break strongholds. Please see prayers below.

### Abortion

*Lord Jesus, I confess aborting my unborn child. I now ask you to forgive me for not protecting my baby and the precious life You entrusted me with. Forgive me for allowing the enemy to convince me that abortion was the only answer. I choose now to dedicate my unborn child to You, and I recognize that I will always be this child's (mom/dad). I know I will meet my baby in heaven. I commit this child into Your hands, Lord Jesus. I forgive myself for choosing death over life. I ask my unborn child's forgiveness for not being a proper guardian of life. Thank you, Jesus, for setting me free from the bondage of my guilt, shame, and blame. In Jesus' Name, amen.*

### Addictions

*In the name of Jesus Christ I command the spirit of addiction to leave my presence! I declare the addiction of _____ (name addictions such as alcohol, street drugs, prescription drugs, food, etc) to be bound by the authority of Jesus Christ. I am free from the slavery of addiction, and I break all satanic connections. Forgive me Jesus for going to outside sources for comfort rather than the comfort of the Holy Spirit. I am no longer a slave to addiction; I am now free by the blood of Jesus! In Jesus' Name, amen.*

### Depression

*In the name of Jesus Christ, I command the spirit of depression and anxiety to leave my presence. I choose to believe that I am blessed and my life is not a mistake. My life has a purpose and a plan. I am*

*hereby God's will with an assignment. I refuse to believe the lie that life is hopeless, and I declare the Truth. "For I know the plans I have for you declares to Lord, plans to prosper you not to harm you plans to give you a hope and a future" (Jeremiah 29:11).*

### Suicidal Ideations

*In the name of Jesus, I bind the demonic spirit of depression, confusion, spiritual apathy, shame, hiding, justification of sin, suicide, death, romanticism of death, and hopelessness to the spirit of depression.*

*In the name of Jesus, I am covered by the protection of His blood. I am covered with the very blood that was shed to give me a life that is glorious. Lord, open my ears and eyes to see what I need to see from You to get through this.*

### Gossip/Cursing

If you have gossiped or slandered people in the past or present, I would like you to take this time and ask God to forgive you. Please list the names of people you have slandered, thus speaking death over, and decide today to speak life! This is a powerful exercise in setting yourself free from captivity by choosing to ask God to bless them and to remove the curse you have spoken over them. Remember that you are to love others as Christ has loved you, and in the end, love is the greatest weapon against Satan. Love always wins!

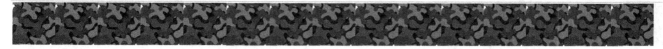

List the people you have gossiped about or cursed:

| Person's Name | Gossip or Curse Spoken |
|---|---|
|  |  |
|  |  |
|  |  |
|  |  |
|  |  |
|  |  |
|  |  |
|  |  |

<u>Please speak this prayer over those you have cursed:</u>

*Dear Jesus, I ask you to cleanse my tongue from all evil and unrighteousness to include gossip and slander. I confess that I have been a mouthpiece for the enemy rather than a mouthpiece for your kingdom. I have not loved others as you have loved me. In your presence, Lord, I now choose to speak life and use my tongue to bring forth life and not death. I now ask You to forgive me for speaking _____(gossip) over_____ (name) and ask you to break the spiritual chain of gossip over my life so I may be free. Please bless those I have cursed in the Name of Jesus. I now pray these curses be broken off their lives. In Jesus' Name, amen!*

<u>Renounce Curses Spoken over you:</u>

*In the name of Jesus Christ I renounce the all curses that were spoken over me such as _____(Name them) (Crazy, Fat, worthless, you are just like you mom/dad, whore, bitch, etc... I break these spoken curses in the name of Jesus and I declare that I am who Christ says I am, and His truth sets me free. I am holy, I am fearless, I am worthy, I am bought with a price and belong to God, I am healed, I have the sound mind of Christ, and I have authority in Christ to defeat the enemy. I am one with Christ and my future belongs to God.*

<u>Renouncing the Spirit of Pride</u>

*"Do you see a man who is wise in his own eyes? There is more hope for a fool than for him." (Proverbs 26:12). "Everyone who is arrogant in heart is an abomination to the Lord; be assured, he will not go unpunished." (Proverbs 16:5). "For if anyone thinks he is something, when he is nothing, he deceives*

*himself." (Galatians 6:3).* Pride is a sin and makes us vulnerable to Satan. If we boast, we are to boast in the Lord, for anything great in us is only great because of Christ. Boast in Him alone. Pride is confidence in ourselves and not in the Lord. Humility is confidence in Christ. Please ask the Lord to reveal ways in which you have been prideful and then say the following prayer aloud.

| Ways I have Been Prideful | |
|---|---|
|  |  |
|  |  |
|  |  |
|  |  |
|  |  |
|  |  |

*Lord Jesus, please reveal to my mind my prideful ways. Forgive me for_____ (list all prideful ways). Your word says that pride goes before a fall. Forgive me for placing confidence in myself rather than being humble by putting my confidence in You. I choose to be Your humble servant. I cast the spirit of pride off me and my bloodline! I declare the power of humility in my life. The humble shall inherit the earth! Thank You for Your humility, Lord, by dying a sinner's death although you were a king. In Jesus' Name, amen.*

"NO SOLDIER LEFT BEHIND"

# Field Exercise 12: Freedom Declaration

## Reread letter from God. (Declare freedom.)

Now that you have completed renouncing generational sin, it is time to reread that letter from God. I highly recommend that you tuck your letter away in your war box as well as any other work of accomplishment in the eleven previous exercises. I want to take a moment to point out all the hard work you have accomplished. I believe you are a soldier ready to set others free. Our goal is to make war heroes and to awake the sedated. The victory is won. Raise your sword and never forget the progress that was made. Because of you, your generation and bloodline will experience spiritual freedom.

As part of the final session, please speak this Oath of Commissioning:

## Boot Camp Oath of Commissioning

Well done, thy good and faithful servant, well done! It is finished! Please complete your Oath of Commissioning at this time.

As a way to commission you, I would like you to declare and sign this Oath of Commissioning.

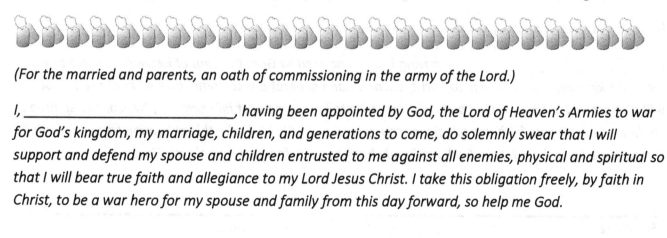

*(For the married and parents, an oath of commissioning in the army of the Lord.)*

*I, _____, having been appointed by God, the Lord of Heaven's Armies to war for God's kingdom, my marriage, children, and generations to come, do solemnly swear that I will support and defend my spouse and children entrusted to me against all enemies, physical and spiritual so that I will bear true faith and allegiance to my Lord Jesus Christ. I take this obligation freely, by faith in Christ, to be a war hero for my spouse and family from this day forward, so help me God.*

_____          _____
*Signature*                                               *Date*

(An oath for singles.)

I, _____, *having been appointed by God, the Lord of Heaven's Armies to war for God's kingdom, my marriage to God, the body of Christ, and my freedom, do solemnly swear that I will support and defend the kingdom of God, my future spouse and my future children entrusted to me against all enemies, physical and spiritual, so that I will bear true faith and allegiance to my Lord Jesus Christ. I take this obligation freely, by faith in Christ, to be a war hero from this day forward, so help me God.*

_____          _____
*Signature*                                               *Date*

(An oath for single parents.)

I, _____, *having been appointed by God, the Lord of Heaven's Armies to war for God's kingdom, my marriage to Christ, children, and generations to come, do solemnly swear that I will support and defend my God and children entrusted to me against all enemies, physical and spiritual, so that I will bear true faith and allegiance to my Lord Jesus Christ. I take this obligation freely, by faith in Christ, to be a war hero for my God and family from this day forward, so help me God.*

_____          _____
*Signature*                                               *Date*

"NO SOLDIER LEFT BEHIND"

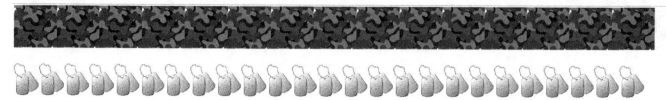

### How to Maintain Freedom

I highly suggest you plug into a church and small group. You need support and not to be isolated. Keep in touch with your Broken No More group or seek individual or group counseling with Maryann at TrainerCounseling@gmail.com . Soldiers that war together, stay together! Use your war box daily. Stay plugged into the Word and don the Armor of God. To don the Armor, I recommend opening your war box and speaking the Word out loud. Be sure to minister to the lost and war for others. Submitting to God is crucial to you maintaining freedom. Remember God said, *"Therefore submit unto God first, then resist the enemy and he will flee from you" (James 4:7).* Maintain your freedom by going back through your field exercises. Cleanse your house daily and fast and pray in your prayer language when more power is needed. Last but not least, align your mind daily with His Word to ensure you are living in truth, not lies.

I want to close with how proud I am for all your efforts in participating in such intense training. You are a war hero. Never forget your position, and never forget your identity. You just changed a bloodline, and you are free! John 8:36 says, "Whom the Son sets free, is free indeed."

Your tombstone now states, "War Hero!"

# "*IT IS FINISHED!!*"

Why? Because there was One Soldier who was and still is the greatest war hero that died on our behalf. And today, because of His blood—holy, sacred, warrior blood—He freed all future soldiers and paved the way on the cross through death for our freedom. Soldier, you are Broken No More in Christ! It is finished! You have won!

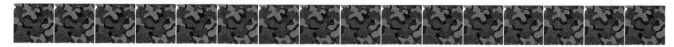

# Support

We highly recommend maintaining your freedom by staying in the Word and plugging into a church family. Do not withdraw or become isolated. The Army of God wars together, not alone.

We also recommend you connect to a Trainer Counseling group program. This assists you in maintaining your freedom. Please email TrainerCounseling@gmail.com to inquire about our counseling programs or for a counseling appointment and further information.

Want to bring this counseling intensive Boot Camp to your church or provide a Boot Camp for your friends or family? Invite Maryann Trainer to speak at your next event or have Maryann provide a Boot Camp for your church, family, small group, etc. E-mail TrainerCounseling@gmail.com or call the office at 937-369-3581. We look forward to setting captives free!

Printed in the United States
By Bookmasters